THE WIFE OF BATH

A Transformation

BY DOUGLAS NORTH

CONTENTS

AUTHOR'S PREFACE

I have called this a transformation instead of a translation because my primary purpose is not to give an accurate Modern English equivalent of each word and line of Geoffrey Chaucer's original, which was written in Middle English. Instead, my purpose was to be faithful to the original story and language as much as possible, but principally to preserve the spirit of the character of The Wife of Bath herself while transforming her into a modern, in fact modern American, voice. Ultimately Alison's personality is center stage in this transformation. Instead of the exact words that make up a translation, her language sounds familiar and has some comic flow.

Sometimes I thought of her as a precursor of today's modern woman comic, perched on a stool instead of a horse and talking to an audience rather than a company of pilgrims. She is also a foremother of The Vagina Monologues.

In brief I wanted her to come alive to a contemporary American audience, while still being painstakingly authentic to the original woman created 600 years ago by her formidable author. Oh yes, and I didn't think that could be done without writing in couplets, because much of the wit of The Wife of Bath's Prologue, is delivered in the well chosen rhymes of the couplet form. Chaucer was a master of the couplet, as were Alexander Pope, Lord Byron, and Dr. Seuss. I am indebted to all of them in this transformation.

I didn't think recreating the Wife of Bath in her Prologue could be accomplished in couplets without some wiggle room. I have taken many liberties, great and small, but all on purpose. There are many lines that do not strictly abide by regular length and meter. But the reader I believe will always have the feeling that it is written in couplets, with the sense of comic cleverness which accompanies that form.

Altogether different literary forms are easily spotted in parts of this trans-formation, and I hope this works. In these sections I rework the original into, for instance, a series of stand-alone proverbs, or a stand-up Hee-Haw joke between two Roman husbands over a back fence, or a dialogue between The Wife and her Fifth Husband to give a sense of how they argued with each other. I hope these departures help transform The Wife of Bath into a recognizably modern woman with a more modern lingo, but who is an accurate representation of the spirit and voice of the original.

I also employ some purposeful anachronisms. Why can't a transformation use a bit of magical realism? No, the Wife of Bath could not have said, "C U next week." But in this transformation, she can, so that her spirit can talk to us now. If you don't find it funny and touching, then I have failed. Chaucer is a deft comic writer, full of complexity and wit as he portrays the social types of his time. He can instantly drop from broad humor and subtle irony into touching seriousness. I try to keep up with that in spirit as best I can.

Basically, I just wrote it down as it flowed out, without consciously exercising any theory of translation at all. It was written in a week in mid-March 2020, when we were all socially distanced, or quarantined, or terrified for our lives and the lives of others. It gave me solace, a little oblivious-ness, and purpose during trying times. I would not have continued with it if Ellen Cole, my wife who is spiritually related to the Wife of Bath and a Pisces, had not laughed with some regularity reading it.

When a modern person thinks of the late Middle Ages, the social type of an arch-feminist does not usually come to mind. Yet here she is. A girl married at twelve who loves, hates, deceives, and manipulates her five husbands over a thirty-some-odd year period of time and ends up rich and powerful, and full of herself. She represents accurately the growing rights of women that accompanied the rise of the middle class in England. Above all I hope this archetypal woman becomes more accessible to people now.

I can imagine a few audiences:

- A modern casual reader who has never read Chaucer (and wouldn't). But she just picks it up (or

loads it down) and has a satisfying read, getting to
know The Wife of Bath and her story;

- A student in a class reading Chaucer who finds the
  language of a rote translation stultifying and just
  isn't enjoying it,
- A student in a class reading it in the original
  Middle English who doesn't get the flow and
  essence of The Wife herself or of her Prologue. But
  once gained, that understanding could be backward
  engineered into the original.
- An English teacher who thinks I tried really hard
  to be both accurate and faithful, and who enjoys it
  enough to think it was worth a few bucks.

It was fun for me to catch up with some of the scholarly
research and analysis of The Wife of Bath's Prologue. The
only scholarly notes you will find to the text concern a couple
of lines that would make no sense unless you knew the
contemporary events that The Wife of Bath is referring to.

Finally, let me remind you of The Wife of Bath's words to her
audience 600 years ago when asked to tell her tale:

"Gladly," quod she, "sith it may you like.
But that I praye to al this compaignye,
If that I speke after my fantasye
As taketh not agrief of that I saye
For myn entente is nat but for to pleye,"

"Gladly," she said, "I'll give you what you wish.
But to be clear, you all must comprehend
That if I tell all, I will surely bend

The truth a bit. So, listen up everyone!
Remember that we're doing this for fun.

I had fun. If you like it—or don't I guess—let me know what you think.

Doug North
Pooka907@gmail.com

AN INTRODUCTION FOR THOSE
NEW TO CHAUCER

Who is the Wife of Bath?

The Wife of Bath is a character created by Geoffrey Chaucer over 600 years ago. To be precise, it is thought that she was created in 1396 as part of a grand literary idea called *The Canterbury Tales*.

Chaucer imagined a group of 30 or so people, a cross-section of English society at the end of the Middle Ages, who have gathered together to make a trip from London to the city of Canterbury, about sixty miles away. It would take about four days on horseback each way.

Back then it was called a Pilgrimage because the destination was a religious shrine, the tomb of Thomas Beckett, a Christian martyr. Today we would call this a Guided Tour, consisting then, as now, of the Tour Guide and the Customers who have paid to take the tour. In this case the Tour Guide, named Harry Bailey, suggests that to pass the time, each of the "Pilgrims" should introduce themselves and tell a couple of stories on the way out and two more on the way back.

Off they go on a nice Spring day. "Chaucer" is on the trip too, writing his book. First, he gives a thumbnail sketch of each Pilgrim. Here is what he says about The Wife of Bath:

There was a good Wife, who came from near Bath.
We noticed right off she was borderline deaf.
She owned a wool business that wove and then sold
Fine fabrics. Better than Flemish, we were told.

At Mass, she was always the first wife to stand
To give the offering—poised, stately, and grand.
If some parish wife dared attempt to be first,
She'd be met with an angry cold shoulder—or worse.

Her kerchiefs were all of fine linen made,
Ten pounds at least they must have weighed.
Each Sunday she wore them upon her proud head
Her elegant stockings were scarlet and red,
Beneath supple shoes that were clearly brand new.

Her features were bold, with a slight reddish hue.

She'd been socially noteworthy throughout her life
And five times, since childhood, she had been a wife,
To say nothing of others she may have known well.
We'll hear about that when she tells us her tale.

She boasted she'd been to Jerusalem three times

And crossed many rivers and sailed many seas .
She'd been to Boulogne and visited Rome
Spent weeks in Galicia, seen the church at Cologne.
An experienced traveler, her horse was first rate
And ambled along with a smooth stepping gait.

Gat-toothed she was, which her wimple revealed,
A brimmed hat above, as large as a shield.
An overskirt covered those wide hips of hers,
And on her two feet were two very sharp spurs.
Openly friendly, she laughed and joked
About lovers and loving, all kinds of romance—
She'd learned all the steps to that old dance.

Of course, those are not Chaucer's words. Six hundred years
ago people in England spoke and wrote in Middle English, not
modern English. The last three lines in the original Middle
English are:

In felaweshipe wel coude she laughe and carpe
Of remedies of love she knew per chaunce
For she koude of that art the olde daunce.

All the other pilgrims are named by their position or employ-
ment—the Knight, the Pardoner, the Prioress, the Miller, and
so forth. In a sense, The Wife of Bath is a professional wife:
she has made her way through life and made her fortune by
inheriting the possessions of a sequence of husbands. Of all
the Pilgrims she is the most modern and revolutionary. Her
era, the late Middle Ages, saw the rise of the middle class.
Her old husbands were rich tradespeople in the flourishing
wool trade of West England. The Wife is even more *avant*

garde because she is a woman. She gained power by taking advantage of new laws that gave widows control of their husbands' wealth and businesses. She became skilled in the business of marriage. She is now a powerful, rich woman who did not inherit her wealth and power from her parentage as did women of the aristocracy. She gained it through her wits and dominating personality—as you will see.

Who is the Pardoner?

The only other Pilgrim with a role in this part of *The Canterbury Tales* is the Pardoner. It is a small role here, but he gets his turn later to introduce himself and tell a tale. He is a religious charlatan who makes his living by going from town to town, pardoning people's sins in exchange for money. That is, he sells tickets to Heaven. He also deals in the sale of religious relics. He interrupts The Wife, telling her to stop preaching about men and marriage and get on with her tale. The Wife puts him in his place, but I believe she also accepts some of his wine, and that loosens her tongue. She tells all.

Why is the First Part All About the Bible?

The Wife starts off talking about the subject of marriage. The reader can assume that the topic of marriage has already come up among the Pilgrims. The Wife enters enthusiastically upon the topic, and after she is done several other Pilgrims speak about marriage. She certainly knows a lot on the topic. She's been married five times and her first marriage was to an old man when she was only twelve. So, she starts off by saying that her lengthy experience makes her an authority on the subject. But of course she can't really be called an authority, because church*men* have made all the rules on marriage, and sexuality, and relationships. She starts quoting from the New and Old Testament and humorously twisting the interpretation to represent her point of view, just as churchmen have twisted the meaning to represent their point of view. The church's official point of view is that virginity is spiritual and pure, women and sexuality are "fallen" but a necessary evil, and women should not marry more than once or be granted their dead husband's estate.

After quite a bit of this, The Pardoner interrupts, The Wife has a nip or two of wine, and proceeds to tell the story of her five marriages.

❧ I ❧
MEN JUST DON'T GET IT

❧ I ❧

THE WIFE ADDRESSES THE
PILGRIMS ON THE SUBJECT OF
HER CREDENTIALS

Experience has taught me a thing or three,
Although, of course, I'm no *Authority*.

I know what goes wrong in the marriage bed,
Because, ladies and gentlemen, I have been wed
Ever since I was twelve—to five different men.

Some *Authorities* think I've been living in sin.
But I thank God in heaven, forever alive,
For each of these *upstanding* husbands, all five.
As I said, there's a question if I can be
Married this often legitimately.

Just yesterday one of you told me that Christ
Attended a marriage once only—not twice—
In all the years He preached in Galilee.
Thus this *symbolic teaching*, you told me,
Means that I must marry only one time.

THE WIFE CONTESTS MEN'S MARRIAGE LAWS

Really? Here's another: Once, the Divine
Jesus sat beside a woman at a well,
A Samaritan no less, and He did tell
Her clearly that since she'd given her hand
Five times, she wasn't married to her current man.

Well, I'm not sure exactly what He meant. I've
Wondered, what was wrong with Number Five?
And was there nothing wrong with Number Four?

Or is the limit three and then no more?

❧ 3 ❧

SHE IS TIPSILY INTERRUPTED BY THE PARDONER

What's that? You ask how many *I* think?

You know, I've never formed a distinct
Answer to *how many*. But I do know *why*.
Men can speculate up and downright lie,
But God made us to thrive and multiply.

THE WIFE CONTINUES HER ARGUMENT WITH A TELLING EXAMPLE

Jesus clearly said that husbands should forego
Their fathers and mothers, and to the altar go.
But not once did he indicate how frequently
These marriages could legitimately be.

The more the marrier I say, tee-hee.
If twice is bigamy, what's eight, octogamy?

Let us consider the wise King, Sir Solomon.
Didn't *he* just have a few wives! I, for one,
Wish I could get it *half* as often. He
Gave God's Gift to Women all his life.
Nobody these days frolics with his wife.
Yeah, King Solomon took many a merry bite
Of every wife on each first night.

5

THE WIFE CONFIDES THAT SHE IS LOOKING. THE APOSTLE PAUL IS OK WITH THIS.

I am glad that I have had my five.
Number 6? I'll know when Mr. Next arrives.
I have no plans to stay chaste and single.
If my ex had died last week, I'd probably mingle,
And Mr. Maybe Right might just appear.
I suppose that this could happen here.
How do I know?
The Apostle tells me so.
He says that I am free
To wed as it pleases me:
"If it's for sex that you constantly yearn
It's better far to marry than to burn."

❧ 6 ❧

FURTHER ARGUMENTATION,
WITH A CAST OF PATRIARCHS

Lamech is the Bible poster boy for Bigamy.
Cursed for having two wives, he lives in infamy.

But what about Abraham! You *know* he was holy.
Likewise Jacob. May I point out coldly
That both of them had more than two wives?
So there!
Bigamous holy men are everywhere.

In fact, is there a single place, a single one,
Where God says marriage is one and done?

SHE NOW TURNS TO
CHURCHMEN'S LOVE OF
VIRGINITY, LEADING TO A
QUESTION

Where did God ever clearly indicate
That virginity is the preferable state?
Apostle Paul? Well, I have clearly read
That when Paul was asked about maidenhead
He admitted he knew no law. Instead,
Let me put it to you this way:

If men advise virginity, that's ok.
But let's just not confuse what they advise
With laws. Perhaps for *them* it's wise.

God on High, he left it up to us,
So let's not legislate or self-distrust.

If He'd commanded total maidenhead
Then there would be no marriage bed.
And with no seed implanted in that row,
Just how exactly would those virgins grow?

❦ 8 ❦

THE WIFE FURTHER
DISTINGUISHES HERSELF FROM
ST. PAUL

St. Paul, to say the least, should not demand,
What Christ Himself neglected to command.
Virginity's been set up like a prize,
A virtue in men, required of maiden wives.
Win it, admire it, set it on your table:
It's upstairs in the house that I'm more able.

These are no idle words. God spoke with passion.
St. Paul? He was on a Virgin's mission.
So he wrote books and preached it was a sin
For folks to live unless they lived like him.

However strong his words, they're just advice—
Not seriously meant for daily life.
So please don't judge some man who marries me,
A freshly widowed woman. It's just not bigamy.
A woman was something Paul would not touch--
Certainly not in bed or on a couch—

He saw peril in a torch near tar and feathers.
Remember France? You need some safety measures.

Note: *The Wife is referring to an actual event that happened three years earlier at the French Court, where some noblemen and King Charles V were dressed up in suits to look like birds. Then they caught fire. It was called the "Bal des Ardents." Wikipedia has a good article on it, including an illustration by Froissart.*

To sum it up, Paul worshipped virginity—
More perfect than marriage with its frailty

Frailty thy name is me, I guess.
Paul liked perfection. We wives are such a mess.

❧ 9 ☙

SHE PRAISES DIVERSITY OVER PERFECTION

I don't envy them, actually,
Those Virginity Men railing at vile bigamy.
They aspire to be spotless in body and spirit.
Me? I'm proud I've been around a little bit.

You know very well that a Lord in his castle
Doesn't use gold to fashion each vessel.
Some are of wood. They too receive praise.
God calls to us in various ways,
Giving us each a special gift.
Here some that, and there some this.

Virginity, that's a kind of perfection.
Like continence. Like devotion.
But Christ, from whom all perfections flow,
Never meant for every John or Joe
To sell it all and give it to the poor
Or quit the world to be Christ's follower.

Paul spoke to the perfectionists of that day.
Ladies and Gentlemen, is that me? No way.
I bring my ripened flowers to the feast
And love my husband 'til he is deceased.

🪰 10 🪰

SHE NOW QUESTIONS THE
PILGRIMS ON THE SUBJECT OF
OUR GENITALIA

Speaking of which, have you ever heard of anyone
Who knew why we have, um,
Organs of generation?

Or why everybody's are so beautifully shaped?
Trust me, their purpose has not escaped
This wife.

Some will hold forth and indicate
Their purpose is to urinate.
They say our little packages down there
Are just to tell the boys from girls. I swear,
Some think that's all.
What? You boys say no?
I think we all agree that isn't so.

The clergy on this outing may be getting hot,

So let me try to clarify this thought.
They are both useful and pleasing too
They make it fun to procreate;
God likes it when we do.

MORE ABOUT GENITALIA AND CHASTITY

Why do famous writers make it clear
That husbands owe a debt to their dear
Wives?

How must the husband make his full payment?
Well, it involves that happy little instrument.
Therefore—here we have a clear demonstration:
They're both for urine and for procreation.

Now I'm not saying every guy who comes provided
With the equipment I have here described
Ought to go use it to make a baby.
A world without *some* chastity is maybe
Lessened. I mean, Christ was a virgin although endowed
As a man. And many a saint was likewise proud
Of being manly, although chaste.

Yet, to me virginity is such a waste.

❧ 12 ❧

A CONCLUDING IMAGE

Let saintly men use perfectly white flour, and instead
We wives will eat that rough-ground barley bread.

PS, Saint Mark notes that barley bread, so crude,
Lord Jesus chose to feed the multitude.

❧ 13 ❧

HER VIEWS ON SEX IN MARRIAGE,
A LIGHT NOTE

Whatever place in life God's named for me,
I will be faithful to it. No, I'm not shy.
In wifehood I will use my instrument
To play God's music as was His intent.

If I play hard to get, God make me pay.
So Husband! You will get it night and day,
Just tell me when you want to pay your debt.
I never have turned down a husband yet.

❧ 14 ❧

BUT THEN A DARKER NOTE

He then becomes my debtor and my slave.
I slowly teach him how he should behave
To give me pleasures owed me as his wife.
I have the upper hand then. Thus through life
I dominate their bodies.
They never knew
I only did what Saint Paul told me to.
He commanded husbands: love them well!
Now there's a rule I've learned how to compel.

✤ 15 ✤

SHE IS RUDELY INTERRUPTED BY
THE PARDONER, WHO IS STILL
DRINKING AND IS REBUFFED

Then the Pardoner stood up and butted in:
"My Lady," said he, "By God you've been
Quite the preacher on this subject. I was
About to take a wife this year. Alas,
Now that I know the price my flesh would pay
I think I'll wait until some future day."

"My tale has not begun," she said, "Hush up.
Just wait, and you'll be sipping a new cup
Of wine before I'm through,
And it will taste as bitter as cheap brew.
When I 've expertly served you up my tale
Of marriage, your cheerful flesh will pale.

Let me make it clear. I have been The Whip.
So from *that* beverage do you care to sip?
Be warned—if you approach too close,
You might not want a spouse. You'll need a nurse.

THE WIFE CONTINUES TO GO TOE TO TOE WITH THE PARDONER, BUT URGES THE COMPANY TO LIGHTEN UP

I will provide examples—more than ten.
If you can't learn from other men
Then by those men you will corrected be,
I learned that from the great Ptolemy.
You can read it in his *Almageste*."

"My Lady, your scholarship I had not guessed.
Now, I hope and pray you'll just begin,"
The Pardoner said, "Spare not the truth. Young men
Must know your clever practices and tricks."

"Gladly," she said, "I'll give you what you wish.
But to be clear, you all must comprehend
That if I tell all, I will surely bend
The truth a bit. So, listen up everyone!
Remember that we're doing this for fun!"

(*Here the Wife of Bath Takes a Drink, or Two*)

❧ II ❧
HER FIRST THREE HUSBANDS

❧ 17 ❧

THE WIFE, FEELING IT, SPILLS
THE BEANS

Now, Sir, *now* I will begin *my* Tale.

I always spill the beans after a wine or ale,
You'll hear the truth. Those husbands that I had?
Three of them were good and two were bad.
The three good men were rich and old.
They could barely make it into bed
Much less fulfill their husband's debt.
You *know* precisely what I mean.

Ha-Ha. I have to laugh. It was a scene.
How every night I'd make them work.
It mattered not to me if some old jerk
Was trying so hard to give me pleasure.
He'd already given me all his land and treasure.
I didn't have to wage a big campaign
To win their love or even hide disdain.

That's how much they loved me. Oh my God,
I laughed within and simply rode roughshod.

❧ 18 ❧

MORE BEANS ARE SPILLED

A wise woman will always have a plan
To get men's love, yes, even when she has none.
But since I had them in the palm of my hand
And since they had given me their land,
I didn't really have to go out of my way.
I didn't try to please them every day.
I gave them nightly workouts, keeping score,
Until they cried out, I am done, no more.

PS, Speaking of Dunmore:
My husbands would not win the bacon
For loving their home life—unless they were faking.

Note: *The Village of Dunmore awarded a prize each summer to the married couple that had the most harmonious marriage in the previous year. The prize was a flitch of bacon.*

❧ 19 ❧

BUT SHE DOES HAVE AN
EDUCATIONAL PURPOSE

I governed them completely with my laws.
They'd race down to the fair to buy gewgaws.
They'd get all teary at my mere kind word.
God knows, the opposite was usually heard.

So listen, you young wives, and listen well,
Here's how you make their lives a living hell.
Please understand that you can make them squirm
And doubt themselves at every single turn.
When it comes to lying, there's no man
Can twist the truth as woman can.

AFTER ALL, SHE WAS MARRIED AT
TWELVE TO AN OLD MAN

I'm not saying this for wives already wise
Though even they must sharpen up their lies.
A teenage wife who knows what's good for her
Will practice how to fool her old *monsieur*.
For instance, tell him how a cowbird's acting crazy
Then get corroboration from Maid Daisy
Whose testimony has been prearranged.

    Or like this:

"You doddering fool, are you deranged?
Our neighbor's wife is honored everywhere
The town awaits the clothing that *she'll* wear.
Meanwhile, here I sit at home, ashamed
Of my drab duds—and who's to blame?
It's you. And where are you? Next door!
You find *her* attractive? Not *me* anymore?
I saw you whispering with Daisy. Dearest God,

Sir Dirty Old Man, cut it out, you clod.

Meanwhile, if *I* should innocently spend
An hour, or two, with some dear friend
You accost me falsely like a fiend,
Heaven forbid that *I* should ever go
To *his* place for some pleasantries: Oh no,
You have to go out and get stinking drunk
Then preach about my crimes.
Ps. He was a hunk.

HOW HER OLD HUSBANDS PREACHED AGAINST WOMEN AND UNFAITHFUL WIVES

You tell me how a bridegroom's never won.
He marries some *poor* girl, it costs a ton.
But if she comes from wealth and family,
She moodily disdains his family tree.

The lovely bride? She too you denigrate
Because foul men like you will salivate.
She'll let herself be wooed and fall.
You say that beauties prove unfaithful, all.

You state men love us 1) for cash
2) for our curves, and 3) for our fair face.
It also helps to sing or dance with grace.
Some have nobility and some can flirt
Here slender arms, there little hands, no dirt.

You conclude, Each virtue is its own downfall.

BY DOUGLAS NORTH

Sooner or later every castle wall
Comes down when it's constantly assaulted.

❧ 22 ❧

THEY ARGUE. HE DOESN'T TRUST
EVEN HOMELY WOMEN

Husband: The homely girl thinks every man exalted
She leaps upon them like a shelter dog
Until some day one buys her, a cheap broad.

The plain gray goose upon the lake
Will find a way to finally find a mate.
How troublesome this urge is to control
This urge all women have, both fair and foul.

Wife: Thus you foolishly insult me in our bed
Saying that wise men really shouldn't wed,
Especially if heaven is what they'd like.
May thunderclaps and fiery lightning strike
And break in two your skinny, withered neck!

Husband: Three things cause men to run for their lives:
dripping ceilings, smoking walls, and scolding wives.

Wife: Run for their lives? For goodness sake,
Why can't an old man give his wife a break?

THE ARGUMENT CONTINUES

Husband: Before the marriage, you girls show nary
a sin.
Once safely married, you let your husbands in
On the truth.

Wife: That's the basic plan
By which we women trap our stupid men.

Husband: Donkeys, oxen, hounds and horse
All these men inspect first, of course,
A basin, a washbowl—never bought unseen.
A spoon, a stool, in fact most anything—
Pots, clothes, apparel—you try them off the rack.
But wives not so. We leap and then we look.

Wife: Surprise, surprise, without a doubt,
Once married, all our vices bubble out.

❧ 24 ❧

AND CONCLUDES AS THE WIFE
HAS THE LAST WORD

Husband: You make a horrid frown and pout
Unless I always point your beauty out.
Unless I gaze admiring on your face,
At parties and events, I'm in disgrace.
Oh, and your birthday! Better not forget
A party, flowers, presents—a banquet.

Wife: Yes, and above all be respectful to my nurse,
And at my chambermaid you must not curse
Honor my father's folks and close Allies
Now be quiet you old barrelful of lies.

✴ 25 ✴

BUT STARTS UP AGAIN, AS
FIGHTS DO

Wife: What *of* our apprentice, Jake? He's so divine,
With his curly hair of spun gold—oh so fine.
Just because he squires me up and down,
You get all jealous and have suspicions.
He's *not* my type. Get over it! You know,
You have no trust, much to my sorrow.

You shouldn't hide that strongbox key!
You know that half its gold belongs to me.
Just how stupid do you think I am?
I swear to God and Good St. James,

Go and get angry! You will never be
Master of all I own *and* master of me.
You must give up one. Case closed, ok?

And why all these questions and spying today?

Sometimes you act like you'd love me the best
Locked in your inmost security chest.

26

THE WIFE HAS SOME ADVICE FOR
OLD HUSBANDS

Here's what you *should* say: "Wife, go where you please.
I won't listen to gossip, be free as a breeze.
I wont listen to malice; I love my Dame Alice."

We wives love no man who needs to take charge
Of our every step; we like to live large.

I've mentioned that ancient and wise Ptolemy.
Whose *Almageste* explicates astrology.
He relates there a proverb that I find so true
That I'd like to share this wisdom with you.

"Of all men living, the wisest is he
Who cares not a whit who the powerful be."

If you have enough, then why should you care
When others are also enjoying a share?
For certain, old dummy, if I may be so bold,

You get lots of vajayjay for someone so old.
How stingy a man who would grimly require
That nobody's candle be lit from his fire.
His own light is constant! It clearly won't rob him!
If he gets enough, then where is the problem?

27

THEY HAVE DIFFERING OPINIONS
ON CLOTHING

You say that young women love to dress gaily,
Adorning themselves with silks and jewels daily,
Thus putting in peril their dear chastity.
What's worse, you dress up this poor argument
With words the Apostle never quite meant:
"You young wives, I tell you, should always take care
Not to wear finery or to fluff up your hair,
No pearls, no gold, no Outfits by Someone
Instead dress drably, preferably homespun."

I care for this thinking much less than a gnat.

Then you say I behave just like a tabby cat.
Because if a man burns his cat's supple fur,
That cat will always her man's house prefer.
But if the cat's coat is a sleek calico,
That cat will quickly from her master go—

Before dawn of the next day she will have fled.
She'll have mixed with the Toms and caterwauled.

You think that gay clothing will make me leave you?
But I have no gay clothes—they're burlap, Sir Shrew.

❦ 28 ❦

SHE WARNS AGAINST HIRING A
PRIVATE DETECTIVE, MAKING
LISTS OF HER FAULTS, AND
DEVISING OBNOXIOUS
COMPARISONS

Old Fool, what good does it do you to spy?
Go ahead—pray to Argus with his hundred eyes.
Recruit him to be my new bodyguard.
He'll see what I want him to. That won't be hard.
By the time I am finished perplexed he will be.

You say it was formerly thought there were three
Things that bring trouble to men on this Earth,
You say you've discovered a horrible fourth.

Dear Sir Cheapskate, Christ will cut short your life
If you don't stop heading each list with "Bad Wife."
There must be new words you can possibly use.
Enough of bad wife! Find some new bugaboos!

You are fond of comparing our loving to hell
Or to barren land where no water can dwell.
You liken our love to the forest wildfire:

The more they consume, the more they desire,
Until the whole forest is burning or burnt.
Our love is like worms whose chewing has turned
The tree, or a husband, to small piles of dust
So will a wife all her man's mettle rust.

29

SHE EXPLAINS HER STRATEGIES AND HOW SHE ALWAYS GAINED VICTORY

So Gentlemen all, you can now understand
How I handled old husbands and kept my command.

I listened each night to their drunken complaints
And denied everything on the lives of the saints.
I denied Jake and that spree with my niece.
I tormented them and gave them no peace.

Of course I was guilty and they innocent,
But they couldn't prove it, and I came and went.
Like an unbroken horse I would bite and I'd whinny.
I turned their complaints back upon them. If any
Dared plot to diminish my freedom and power
I'd threaten them first. First to mill gets the flour.

❧ 30 ❧

HOW SHE ALWAYS WON THE WAR

My first volley ended our marital war:
They ran from the field i.e. backed out the door.
I pursued them with false accusations of wenches
Until, sick and tired, they abandoned their trenches.

Yet somehow I managed to tickle their hearts.
One even believed I was searching for tarts
Who had quenched his odd lusts.
When I left for the night.
He showed no distrust.
As you can imagine, it tickled me too.
I'd laugh. This was what I was born to do.
Deceit, weeping, acting, using my guiles.
God put wiles in women—in our eyes, in our smiles.

One thing I boast of—feel free to repeat it—
The Wife of Bath has never been defeated.

By trickery or force, or by some sort of thing
Like mumbling to myself or continually grousing,
I got my way. I was particularly nasty in bed.
Grouchy, unpleasant, I'd play hard to get.
If I felt his arm on me, I'd push it away;
If he pressed on, I'd get up straightaway.
All this to weasel some goodies from him.
He'd give it me; then I'd give it to him.

HER UNDERSTANDING OF THE
WAY OF THE WORLD

I love to tell this maxim to a male:
Either sex can win when everything's for sale.

You can't lure hawks with nothing in your hand
To win I suffered lusts I really couldn't stand.
I'd act as if he'd sent me to the moon
But I was hoping he would finish soon.

Even had the Pope come by for dinner
I would have cursed my husband as a sinner.

In truth, with men I've traded word for word
I swear it here before Almighty God
If I were to write my will today
There'd be no final insults left to say.

❧ 32 ❧

THE IMPORTANT ROLE OF CHARM

I've made my way by using my wits,
They always gave in because I gave them fits.
They'd roar like a lion on each such occasion
Then bleat like a lamb with some friendly persuasion.

It would go down like this: "Sweetheart, do you see
How our sheep Willy behaves timidly?
Come here, dear husband, let me kiss your dear cheek.
I would love it if *you* could just be that meek.
You frequently preach about Job's faithful trust
Well, you could be milder and learn to adjust.
Be flexible. Practice what you preach,
If you don't, naughty boy, I will teach
You a lesson. Let your wife live in peace."

❧ 33 ❧

AND HARD BARGAINING

One of us two has to bow, there's no doubt,
And since men are better at thinking things out
Than women, I think that *you'd* be the one
To give way graciously like the moon to the sun.

Why do you fume and pull out your hair
Do you *need* to own all of my body down there?
Well go ahead, take it—all, every bit
But by God you'd better adore all of it.

You know, if I wish, I can lead the rich life
If I sell my *belle chose*; it will fetch a high price.
But I'll keep my rosebud for your eyes alone,
Since you've admitted that you were so wrong.

That's how we spoke; I kept them in hand.
Now I will tell of my fourth husband.

❦ III ❦
HER FOURTH HUSBAND

❦ 34 ❦

HER WILD YEARS

My fourth husband reveled in parties and drink.
And he had a girl on the side, I think—
In fact, I know. But what did I care?
I was young and making the scene everywhere.
Stubborn and strong, babbling on like a magpie,
No one could dance to the small harp like I.
I was known for my singing—a sweet nightingale—
When I had drunk too much wine or dark ale.

Metallius, that old Roman pervert, that swine,
He murdered his wife because she drank wine.
He beat her with his cane. Now if I'd been his wife
And he kept me from drinking, *he'd* lose his life.

My thoughts turn to Venus whenever I drink:
And as sure as the cold will be followed by hail,
My liquorous mouth stirs my lecherous tail.

BY DOUGLAS NORTH

And when women get drunk, they lose their defense,
And lechers all know this from experience.

35

A TOUCHING REVERIE SWEEPS
THE WIFE AWAY

But, Christ, recollecting those years and that boy,
My gay youth. It moves me to tears of joy.
My heart root tingles. We were all so gay.
And it starts beating fast, yes even today,
Because in my time I danced with my world.
Now age has me bent and my fingers are curled.
I'm bereft of my beauty, my spirit, my revels.
Let it go, fare thee well, now go to the devil!
The flour is gone. What more is there to tell?
The bran, as best I can, I now must sell.

But I'll get by and get on happily.

Where was I? My fourth husband? OK, let's see.

✢ 36 ✢

A NEW WAR A NEW STRATEGY

Yes, he curdled my heart. I was jealous and swore
Revenge at the thought that he might love her more.
But I got even, by God and Saint Joyce
I took the same wood and put *him* on the cross.
Not with my body and not through foul play
Instead I threw parties. I was happy and gay.
I fried him in his own fat for a while.
Hot with anger and jealous, he lost his smug smile.

By God, here on earth was his Purgatory.
So he may be in Heaven; that's not up to me.
I know for a fact that down here he felt pain,
For his marriage shoe pinched again and again.

How much he suffered! Only he and God know
The ways I contrived to torture him so.
He died when I came back from Jerusalem.
His body lies buried beneath the cross beam.

37

SHE REALLY DID NOT LIKE
THAT GUY

I admit his tomb is not so well engraved
As the sepulcher of Darius, which was made
Exquisite by the noble Appeles.
I should spend that kind of money? Puhleeze!

So fare thee well. God grant your soul relief.
He lies there in his casket, now at peace.

❧ IV ❧
HER FIFTH HUSBAND

❦ 38 ❧

OF DOMESTIC ABUSE AND
LEARNED HELPLESSNESS

Now of my fifth husband will I tell.

I really hope *his* soul won't rot in hell,
Despite the fact I was so badly used.
I'm counting one by one the ribs he bruised.
I'll feel them right up to my dying day,
But in our bed he was so fresh and gay.
That was how he always led me on.
He treated my *belle chose* just like a queen.
Even though he beat my every bone,
I loved him when we were upstairs alone.

39

THE PSYCHOLOGY AND
ECONOMICS OF THE OLDER WIFE

I think I loved him best for only he
In loving was so standoffish to me.

We women have this weakness sexually.
It's one part lust and two parts fantasy.
If there's something—someone—we can't have
Then that's who we will cry out for and crave.
Forbid us anything, that's what we'll seek.
Force something on us? Bye-bye. C U next week.

Hold back and we'll extend our loving hands.
The price goes up at crowded market stands.
When few want what we have, down goes the price.
All women know this. That's why we're called wise.

❦ 40 ❧

SHE MET HIM WHEN SHE WAS
UNHAPPILY MARRIED

This fifth husband of mine: God his soul bless.
I married him for love, for he was penniless.
He was a Clerk at Oxford, as a rule,
But he would come back home when not at school.
He took a room at my best friend's, in town.

God bless her too, named like me, Alison.
I told her all my secret thoughts—at least,
I told her much more than the parish priest.
I held nothing back from her at all.

If my fourth husband, drunk, had pissed the wall,
Or done some stupid thing that risked his life,
I'd tell her and one other gossipy wife,
As well as my niece, both favorite confidants.
I did this to disturb him. What a dunce!
How his face would get red-hot with shame,
That I had shared his secrets with my dames!

❧ 41 ❧

HOW THEY MET DURING HER
MOST PROMISCUOUS WEEKS

It happened that one year, some time around Lent,
My best friend Alice and I often spent
Our days together. All that March, April, and May
From house to house we'd make our way,
Keeping up on the latest gossip and rumors.
But one day Alison and I, and her roomer—
Jankyn—went out in the fields for a walk.

My husband was in London—at a Lenten talk.
I 'd seen this as a chance to play around
A bit, with some of the faster set in town—
Make some new friends, see and be seen—
How little I knew of what gracious fate,
Mysteriously, was now taking shape!

I had started going to Lenten events.
Lots of processions and feasts under tents,
Preachings and some local pilgrimages,

Miracle plays and grand marriages.
I wore gay scarlet robes and sheer red tights.

They were totally free from worms, moths, and mites,
For they were on and off at least twice a day.
Constant use keeps those weevils away.

❧ 42 ❧

HOW SHE SLYLY BAITED A HOOK
FOR JANKYN

But back to my tale, we were out in the lea.
Jankyn the Clerk was flirting with me.
I was, too. And then I saw my chance:
"If I were a widow...." I shot him a glance.

❧ 43 ❧

THE PLEASURE SHE TAKES IN A
WELL DESIGNED PLOT

If there is one thing gets me totally intense
It's when I arrange my own providence.
Don't look for me to play Stupid Mouse
Who has but single door to his house,
And if it's blocked, his life is over.

I acted enchanted, but that was my cover,
A subtle trick I learned from my mother.
I told him that I'd dreamed of him all night.
I dreamed he slew me as I lay upright
And I lay dead in a pool of my blood.

This omen was good, I said, for I'd been told,
That red blood in dreams equals pure gold.
Pure fiction! I never dreamed that dream.
My wise mother aided me often, it seems.

❧ 44 ❧

AFTER A WISTFUL MOMENT WE
ATTEND HER FOURTH HUSBAND'S
FUNERAL

Where was I? My thoughts have wandered away.
It was all so real then. Just a story today.

As my fourth husband's body lay upon his bier,
I never stopped crying, but smiled through my tears.
Wives have to do this; it is *de rigueur.*
Just cover your face and sob for *monsieur.*
My fallback plan had provided a mate.
How little I cried I can't overstate.

My husband was carted to church the next morning.
His neighbors and friends wore expressions of mourning.
Jankyn was among them, and here I must beg
God's forgiveness, I couldn't resist his nice leg,
And his two feet so pretty, so clean and so fair.
My heart didn't notice one other soul there.

✣ 45 ✣

HOW COULD SHE HAVE FALLEN
FOR THIS BOY? WE CONSULT
ASTROLOGY

It was love, and he was but twenty in truth.
I was forty, but I'd always had a colt's tooth.
Gat-toothed I was, and the saying proved true,
For I worshipped Saint Venus, as such people do.
So help me God, I was a lusty gal,
Pretty, rich, still young: I had it all.
(Just between us, my men all said the same:
Down there I put the other gals to shame.)

Venus controls my heart. It's in the stars.
My sturdy spirit? That belongs to Mars.
Taurus my rising sign, Mars lives within.

Alas, alas, that love's considered sin.

✤ 46 ✤

MORE OF ASTROLOGY AND
SEXUALITY

I've always followed my amorous heart,
Compelled by my astrological chart.
I guess that's why I could never refrain
From opening my chamber of Venus to men.

I have the mark of Mars on my red face
And also down there in that privy place.
I hope God on High will save even me,
I gave love to all indiscriminately.

I always followed my fierce appetite;
He could be short or tall, could be black or white.
He could be poor or of poor pedigree,
I took no notice if he pleased me.

✺ 47 ✺

WHAT HAS SHE DONE?

So, what can I say? At the month's end,
That beautiful Clerk? I accepted his hand.
Our wedding was grand. The music was solemn,
All my wealth and my land was now held in common,
All those things I'd collected from husbands before.

I have never regretted anything more.

❧ 48 ❧

CLERKS HAVE A PROBLEM WITH
WOMEN, IT TURNS OUT

He kept me apart from the things I hold dear.
One time he smacked me so hard on my ear
(Because I had torn out a book's precious leaf)
That even today it is totally deaf.
I put up a fight like a wild lioness
But I had no claws, just my sharp cheekiness.

I walked house to house just as I had before
Although he insisted I do that no more.
So then he'd get up on the woodbox and preach
From Latin proverbial stories, to teach
Me a lesson.
Simplicius Gallus divorced his wife;
She got not a cent for the rest of her life.
She was looking out from his front door,
Looking out bareheaded that is, nothing more.

Another Roman (the name I can't recall)
His wife went all alone to a summertime ball
She too was divorced, and got nothing at all.

49

LOTS OF PROBLEMS LOTS OF
MISOGYNIST READINGS.

Then he'd search in his Bible for *Ecclesiastes*,
And his favorite part where the prophet decrees
That men must not let their wives wander out.

Then he'd turn to his next-favorite text, without doubt:
"Men who build houses from thin willow branches,
Or gallop blind horses on turf, take their chances.
So too with the husband who pilgrimages allows:
Such foolish men should be hanged in the gallows."

Like I was listening! I flipped off his laws
And his stories, and maxims and moldy old saws.
I told him I must always be free.
I hate men who feel they must discipline me.

"And I am not the only wife who feels so caged!"
This made him turn purple he was so enraged.
He knew that I hated him. We were at war.

🏵 50 🏵

JANKYN'S BOOK OF WICKED
WOMEN

By the way, remember that leaf that I tore
From his precious book? And he gave me a blow
That made my ear useless from then until now?

He loved to read books out loud night and day.
Just for his sport he would read one always:
It was called *Valerie and Theophraste*.
Whenever he read it I cringed and he laughed.

It held treatises, one by a clerk from old Rome
A cardinal whose name was Saint Jerome,
Whose piece was called *Against Jovinian*,
Others were Crisippus, Trotula, and Tertullian.
It held just one tract by a woman, Heloise.
Who was an abbess, somewhere near Paris.

The parables of Solomon; the Art of Ovid,
Together they made up his book most beloved,

Each night a favorite treatise he picked,
The subject identical: all wives are wicked.
The Bible has legends of heroic women.
This book specialized in tall tales of our sin.

Take it from me, a Clerk will hate wives
And all but the Saints he will scorn and despise.

彩 51 彩

THE WIFE SHOWS HER PROFOUND UNDERSTANDING OF GENDER POLITICS

Please recall Aesop's fable, "The Man and the Lion,"
If lions could paint, then the *man* would be dying.

Note: *This brief fable is readily available on the Internet.*

So too with women. *We* don't get oratories;
We don't get paid, like a Clerk, to tell stories,
If we did, we could tell of such wickedness,
That all Saints together could never redress.

52

LIFE, FATE, AND ASTROLOGY

I'm a Pisces. Sometimes my Venus has dominion
And Mercury, conversely, is but a minion.

Mercury's all about science and math,
Venus loves luxury, a hot bubble bath.

Each suffers loss from the other's gain:
When Venus is happy then Mercury's pained;
When Venus falls, then Mercury is raised.
Thus women, by Clerks, will never be praised.

53

A DIFFERENT HYPOTHESIS ABOUT
WHY CLERKS WRITE HATELIT

The Clerk, growing old, finds it hard to perform
His duties to Venus as he did before,
And so this old Clerk, he writes his great treatise
About cheating wives and how great their deceit is.

54

BACK TO THAT MISOGYNIST BOOK

But don't get me started! Back to my story
Of books and a beating that made my ear gory.

One night, Jankyn, who now was my Sire,
Read from His Book as he sat by the fire.
Eve was the subject, and her wickedness:
And how it's her fault there's such wretchedness,
Eve mothered the spear that bloodied Dear Jesus:
Without Eve and her sin, there's no need to redeem us.

In this book, as you see, it's expressly defined—
Women get blamed for the Fall of Mankind.

He read to me how Sampson lost his hair,
Snipped by Delilah late one night, with shears.
And how her treason cost him both his eyes.

He read me about Diane and Hercules.

Now please don't laugh or think me a liar:
Di caused Herk to set himself on fire!

He read, in tedious detail, of the strife
That Socrates experienced with each wife.
When Xantippe poured a pisspot on his head.
This meditative man just sat still, then said,
"Before thunder, always comes the rain."
(I have to admit that was a good line.)

HO-HUM. YET MORE OF THESE STORIES

He told of Pasiphae, the Cretan Queen.
He knew this "sweet tale" always perturbed me
Ugh. What she did, what she liked: it disturbed me.

Clytemnestra slept with her brother-in-law.
Then they killed her husband, back from the war.
He told her story with remarkable relish.

Another tale he liked to embellish
Was of Amphiorax. "How did he lose his life?"
He would ask. "Did it perhaps involve his wife?"
She sold him out to the Greeks for some gold,
So they went and got him in his stronghold.
Things got ugly for him then in Thebes I was told.

Lyvia and Lucy—each killed her mate,
But one was for love and one was for hate.
Lyvia used poison and then watched him go.

That's how much she hated her foe.
Lucy adored her man, but got a strange notion.
To make him her love-slave, she bought a love-potion.
He drank it, but he never saw tomorrow.

"Love or hate, either way," he said, "Husbands find sorrow."

❧ 56 ☙
WILL THESE STORIES
NEVER END?

Next on his list was Mr. Latymus,
Leaning over his backyard fence with Arrius.
Mr. L: I have in my garden an unlucky tree.
Mr. A: Oh really? What can the problem be?
Mr. L: My three wives all hanged themselves in despair.
Mr. A: OMG do you have a shoot? Please tell me where.

Later that month he focused on wives
Who used family beds to take husbands' lives—
Some hit the sheets with their lovers that night
With hubby's corpse on the floor in plain sight.
Some deftly drove nails right through his brain
While he slept, and never awakened again.
Some dripped poison in his favorite nightcap.

My heart just couldn't stomach this crap.

❧ 57 ❧

NOW IT'S PROVERBS!

Then he would further delight me with proverbs
A multitude meant to shame and disturb.

"Better live with a lion or love a foul dragon
Than live with a woman who is always ragging."

"Better to live on the roof in the cold
Than in a warm house with a shrew or a scold."

"Women all scheme and use subtle measures
To rob their husbands of life's little pleasures."

"Wives lose their shame along with the frocks
They let slip to the floor as their lover knocks."

"A beautiful girl who's depetaled her rose
Is just like a pig with a ring in its nose."

⚜ 58 ⚜

THE WIFE HAS HAD ENOUGH

Who could suppose or even imagine
The hurt that I felt? It made my heart spin.

When I realized that forever, each night,
My husband would read from that book with delight,
All suddenly I lunged and ripped out three leaves,
Right out of the book, as he read some critique,

And I popped him a good one, right on the cheek.

He fell down backwards into the hearth-fire.
He jumped back up. Now his *eyes* were on fire.
With his right fist he smacked me upside the head.
I went down on the floor *as if* I were dead.

✿ 59 ✿

THE WIFE USES HER MOTHER'S
WILES ON JANKYN YET ONE
MORE TIME

And when he thought me dead on the floor,
He almost panicked and fled through the door,
But I feigned trying to gain consciousness.
"So now you have finally killed me, I guess.
Is it for my land that I murdered be?
Come here, lover boy, one last kiss for me."

He drew near, gently smiling. He slowly knelt down.
"Oh my God, Dear Alison, what have I done?
I swear I'll never hit you again. Really, I rue it.
If only you hadn't driven me to it.
Forgive me, Forgive me, Your pardon I seek."

I hit him again, the same place on the cheek.
"Thief!" I said, "That's for stealing my land.
I grow weak and am dying.
Can't talk, understand?"

❧ 60 ❧

THEY RESOLVE THEIR ISSUES TO
THE SATISFACTION OF THE WIFE
OF BATH

But after a while, after many a fray,
We came to agreement, our order of play.
He gave me the bridle, to hold in my hand,
The governance of all our business and land—
Including, of course, his tongue and his fist.
"You also must burn that book, I insist."

So when I had thus gained complete mastery
And ruled the household in full sovereignty,
He said, "Alison, you are my own true wife.
Do what you please for the rest of your life.
Please, be honorable, think of my reputation.
After that day we enjoyed good relations.

I was to him in every way kinder,
Than any wife from Denmark to China.
I was true to him as he was true to me.

I pray to God Who Sits in Majesty:
Bless that man's soul; he did right by me.

Now I'll tell my tale, if you will hear.

Here Ends The Prologue of The Wife of Bath.

Made in the USA
Middletown, DE
10 May 2021